AMDG

# Glory be to God

A STONYHURST PRAYER BOOK

St Omers Press
*Stonyhurst*

ACKNOWLEDGMENTS

The Stonyhurst Association thanks all those who have helped with this prayer book: the College pupils for their prayers and photographs; the College staff, Claire Oxley and Fintan O'Reilly, who helped with the photography; Stephen Oliver who produced the Appendix notes; Simon Bishop SJ, Philip Endean SJ, Nicholas King SJ, Billy Hewett SJ, Frances Orchard IBVM, and Michael O'Halloran SJ who contributed ideas as to content; and those who brought it all together, Anthony Eyre, Christopher Page, Matthew Power SJ and Beverley Sillitoe. Many others have given encouragement and support. Other prayer books, particularly the previous Association Prayer Book, have been used; every reasonable attempt has been made to check copyright, but if there are oversights please contact the Association.

First published 2003
Reprinted 2007

St Omers Press
3-9 Cripps Road, Cirencester GL7 1HN



ISBN: 978-0-9553592-2-4

Printed in China

# INTRODUCTION

Many of the prayers and reflections in this collection are in regular use at Stonyhurst today. Others will be more familiar to an older generation of OS. Some others have been composed by pupils this year. Together they represent something of the spiritual heritage which enriches the lives of all who have been associated with the College, as pupils, as staff or as parents.

There is the old adage about prayer that one should pray as one can and not as one can't. That said, the structure and lay out of the book is intended to favour what St Ignatius in the *Spiritual Exercises* calls 'The Second Way of Praying', a slow and meditative reading of a prayer. The photographs, of the College and its surroundings, are there to enhance this reflective quality.

The last Association prayer book was published in 1993, the 400th anniversary of the foundation of the College at St Omers. This new prayer book was first published in the year that marked the bi-centenary of the restoration of the British Province of the Society of Jesus at Stonyhurst in May 1803.

It is our hope that this prayer book will assist all those connected with the College 'in ways proportional to their age and maturity' (to use the words of Pedro Arrupe SJ) to develop 'a way of life that is it in itself a proclamation of the charity of Christ, of the faith that comes from him and leads back to him, and of the justice which he announced.'

# AT THE BREAK OF THE DAY

*Lord of all hopefulness, Lord of all joy,*
*Whose trust, ever childlike, no care could destroy,*
*Be there at our waking, and give us we pray,*
*Your bliss in our hearts, Lord, at the break of the day*

Dear Lord, we thank you for bringing us safely to this new day.

*A Rhetorician*

Give us inspiration and enthusiasm in the morning, love throughout the day and forgiveness in the evening.

*A Poet*

In the morning let me know your love, O Lord.

*Psalm 142*

Come, Holy Spirit, fill the hearts of your faithful, and enkindle in them the fire of your love.

Send forth your Spirit and they shall be created:
And you shall renew the face of the earth.

O God, who taught the hearts of the faithful by the light of the Holy Spirit, grant that, by the gift of the same Spirit, we may be always truly wise and ever rejoice in his consolation. Through Christ our Lord.
Amen.

*Prayer to the Holy Spirit*

Rise and shine,
Give God the glory, glory.
Rise and shine,
Give God the glory, glory.
Rise and shine and
Give God the glory, glory,
Children of the Lord.

*Chorus of the song sung at every Stonyhurst Children's Holiday Trust (formerly HLHCT) Week, and at the OS Children's Holidays and at Lourdes. Please remember these works in your prayers.*

O all you works of the Lord, O bless the Lord.
To him be highest glory and praise for ever.
And you angels of the Lord, O bless the Lord.
To him be highest glory and praise forever.

And you, sun and moon, O bless the Lord.
And you, the stars of the heavens, O bless the Lord.
And you showers and rain, O bless the Lord.
To him be highest glory and praise forever.

And you mountains and hills, O bless the Lord.
And you, all plants of the earth, O bless the Lord.
And you fountain and springs, O bless the Lord.
To him be highest glory and praise forever.

And you spirits and souls of the just, O bless the Lord.
And you holy and humble of heart, O bless the Lord.
And you servants of the Lord, O bless the Lord.
To him be highest glory and praise forever.

Let us praise the Father, the Son, and the Holy Spirit:
To you be highest glory and praise forever.

*from Daniel 3*

*Pied Beauty*

Glory be to God for dappled things –
For skies of couple-colour as a brinded cow;
For rose-moles all in stipple upon trout that swim;
Fresh-firecoal chestnut-falls; finches' wings;
Landscape plotted and pieced – fold, fallow and plough;
And all trades, their gear and tackle and trim.

All things counter, original, spare, strange;
Whatever is fickle, freckled (who knows how?)
With swift, slow; sweet, sour; adazzle, dim;
He fathers-forth whose beauty is past change:
Praise him.

*Gerard Manley Hopkins SJ, 1844-1889*

*The Apostles' Creed*

I believe in God, the Father almighty,
Creator of heaven and earth,
And in Jesus Christ, his only Son, our Lord,
Who was conceived by the Holy Spirit,
Born of the Virgin Mary,
Suffered under Pontius Pilate,
Was crucified, died, and was buried.

He descended into Hell.
The third day, he rose again from the dead.
He ascended into heaven,
And is seated at the right hand of the Father.
From thence, he will come to judge
The living and the dead.

I believe in the Holy Spirit,
The Holy Catholic Church,
The Communion of Saints,
The forgiveness of sins,
The resurrection of the body
And life everlasting. Amen.

*The Universal Prayer*

Lord, I believe in you: increase my faith.
I trust in you: strengthen my trust.
I love you: let me love you more and more.
I am sorry for my sins: deepen my sorrow.

I worship you as my first beginning,
I long for you as my last end,
I praise you as my constant helper,
And call on you as my loving protector.

Guide me by your wisdom,
correct me with your justice,
comfort me with your mercy,
protect me with your power.

Let me love you, my Lord and my God,
and see myself as I really am:
a pilgrim in this world,
a Christian called to respect and love
all those whose lives I touch,
those in authority over me,
or those under my authority,
my friends and my enemies.

Help me to conquer anger with gentleness,
greed by generosity,
apathy by fervour.
Help me to forget myself
and reach out towards others.

*Attributed to Pope Clement XI, 1649-1721*

Take, Lord, and receive all my liberty, my memory, understanding, and my entire will – all that I have and call my own. You have given it all to me. To you, Lord, I return it. Everything is yours; do with it what you will. Give me only your love and your grace. That is enough for me.

*St Ignatius Loyola,* Spiritual Exercises *[235]*

Father in heaven, you have given us a mind to know you, a will to serve you, and a heart to love you. Be with us today in all that we do, so that your light may shine out in our lives; through Christ our Lord.

*St Thomas More, 1478-1535*

Most Sacred Heart of Jesus, we place all our trust in you, fearing all in our weakness, hoping all things in your goodness; be alone our love, the protector of our lives, the stay of our weakness, the strengthener in our inconstancy, the repairer of all our faults, the assurance of our salvation and our refuge at the hour of our death. Amen.

*(Anon)*

*Morning Offerings*

O Jesus, through the pure Heart of Mary, I offer you the prayers, works, sufferings and joys of this day, for all the intentions of your Sacred Heart.

*Apostleship of Prayer*

Lord, Creator, Father, may we come to know you better.
Lord, Creator, Father, may we follow in your ways.
Lord, Creator, Father may we use our talents well,
And Lord, Creator, Father may we offer all to you.

Guide us, keep us, help us,
teach us what we need.
Keep us safe from harm
And bless us every day.

*A Poet*

Lord Jesus, I give you
my hands to do your work,
my feet to go your way,
my eyes to see as you do,
my tongue to speak your words,
my mind that you may think in me,
my spirit that you may pray in me.
Above all, I give you my heart
that you may love in me your Father and all mankind.
I give you my whole self
that you may grow in me,
so that it is you, Lord Jesus,
who live and work and pray in me.

*Launcelot Andrewes, 1555-1626*

My God, I believe most firmly that you watch over all who hope in you, and that we can want for nothing when we rely upon you in all things. Therefore I am resolved for the future to cast all my cares upon you.

*St Claude la Colombière SJ, 1641-1682*

*Psalm 139*

O Lord, you search me and you know me,
you know my resting and my rising,
you discern my purpose from afar.
You mark when I walk or lie down,
all my ways lie open to you.

Before ever a word is on my tongue
you know it, O Lord, through and through.
Behind and before you besiege me,
your hand ever laid upon me.
Too wonderful for me, this knowledge,
too high, beyond my reach.

O where can I go from your spirit,
or where can I flee from your face?
If I climb the heavens, you are there.
If I lie in the grave, you are there.

If I take the wings of the dawn
and dwell at the sea's furthest end,
even there your hand would lead me,
your right hand would hold me fast.

If I say: 'Let the darkness hide me
and the light around me be night,'
even darkness is not dark for you
and the night is as clear as the day.

For it was you who created my being,
knit me together in my mother's womb.
I thank you for the wonder of my being,
for the wonders of all your creation.

Already you knew my soul,
my body held no secret from you
when I was being fashioned in secret
and moulded in the depths of the earth.

Your eyes saw all my actions,
they were all of them written in your book;
every one of my days was decreed
before one of them came into being.

To me, how mysterious your thoughts,
the sum of them not to be numbered!
If I count them, they are more than the sand;
to finish, I must be eternal like you.

O search me, God, and know my heart.
O test me and know my thoughts.
See that I follow not the wrong path
but lead me in the path of life eternal.

My Lord God, I have no idea where I am going. I do not see the road ahead of me. I cannot know for certain where it will end. Nor do I really know myself, and the fact that I think I am following your will does not mean that I am actually doing so. But I believe that the desire to please you does in fact please you. And I hope I have that desire in all that I am doing. I hope that I will never do anything apart from that desire. And I know that if I do this, you will lead me by the right road, though I may know nothing about it. Therefore, I will trust you always, though I may seem to be lost and in the shadow of death. I will not fear, for you are with me, and you will never leave me to face my perils alone.

*Thomas Merton, 1915-1968*

*Prayer for the Pope*

Let us pray for our Pope.
May the Lord bless, guide, protect and strengthen him, that, inspired by the Holy Spirit, he may lead us to greater unity, confirm our faith and the faith of our brothers and sisters, and urge us to live more generously as disciples of Jesus Christ, who with the Father and the Holy Spirit lives for ever and ever. Amen.

*Prayers for the Queen*

Domine, salvam fac reginam nostram, Elizabeth: et exaudi nos in die qua invocaverimus te.

I have and I do pray for Elizabeth, your queen and my queen, for whom I wish a long reign and prosperity.

*St Edmund Campion SJ (born 1540, martyred 1st December 1581), last words at Tyburn.*

*Prayer through the intercession of the Blessed St Omers' Martyrs*

Grant, Lord God, that through the merits and the intercession of St Thomas Garnet, St John Plessington, St Philip Evans and the Blessed Martyrs of the College, we may, by your grace and with all the strength that is in us, follow in their footsteps and live and die not unworthy of these glorious predecessors of ours.

We ask this through Christ, Our Lord. Amen.

*A Prayer for Peace*

To you, Creator of nature and humanity, of truth and beauty, I pray . . .

*Hear my voice*, for it is the voice of all the victims of all wars and violence among individuals and nations.

*Hear my voice*, for it is the voice of all children who suffer, when people put their faith in weapons and war.

*Hear my voice*, when I beg you to instil into the hearts of all human beings, the wisdom of peace, the strength of justice and the joy of fellowship.

*Hear my voice*, for I speak for the multitudes in every country and in every period of history, who do not want war and are ready to walk the road of peace.

*Pope John Paul II, 1920-2005*

*Prayer for the Sick*

Father, your Son accepted our sufferings to teach us the virtue of patience in human illness. Hear the prayers we offer for . . .

May all those who suffer pain, illness or disease come to realise that they are chosen to be saints and know that they are joined to Christ in his sufferings for the salvation of the world.

We ask this through Christ our Lord. Amen.

Lord, we pray for those who are sick. We remember in particular those who are greatly burdened by whatever illnesses they have to bare. Give them strength and comfort through the difficult times and fill them with hope. May their anxieties be eased and love showered upon them.
Amen.

*A Poet*

*Morning Prayers*

In the name of the Father and of the Son and the Holy Spirit. Amen.

Lord, open our lips.
And we shall praise your name.

Glory be to the Father,
and to the Son
and to the Holy Spirit.
As it was in the beginning,
is now, and ever shall be,
world without end.
Amen.

*Psalm 99*

Cry out with joy to God, all the earth:
Serve the Lord with gladness.
Come before him, singing for joy.

Know that he, the Lord, is God.
He made us, we belong to him,
We are his people, the sheep of his flock.

Go within his gates, giving thanks.
Enter his courts with songs of praise.
Give thanks to him and bless his name.

Indeed, how good is the Lord,
eternal his merciful love.
He is faithful from age to age.

*Scripture reading*

*Benedictus*
Blessed be the Lord, the God of Israel!
He has visited his people and redeemed them.

He has raised up for us a mighty saviour
in the house of David his servant,
as he promised by the lips of holy men,
those who were his prophets from of old.

A saviour who would free us from our foes,
from the hands of all who hate us.
So his love for our fathers is fulfilled
and his holy covenant remembered.

He swore to Abraham our father to grant us,
that free from fear, and saved from the hands of our foes,
we might serve him in holiness and justice
all the days of our life in his presence.

As for you, little child,
you shall be called a prophet of God, the Most High.
You shall go ahead of the Lord
to prepare his way before him,
to make known to his people their salvation
through the forgiveness of all their sins,
the loving-kindness of the heart of our God
who visits us like the dawn from on high.
He will give light to those in darkness,
those who dwell in the shadow of death
and guide us into the way of peace.

*Concluding Prayers*

Our Father, who art in heaven . . .

True Light of the world, Lord Jesus Christ,
as you enlighten all men for their salvation,
give us grace we pray
to herald your coming
by preparing the ways of justice and peace.

Father of Jesus Christ,
open our hearts to your word
and to the power of the Spirit.
Give us love to discover your will
and strength to carry it out today;
for you are the light for ever and ever.

May Christ, the only Son of God, bless and help us.
Amen.

QUANT IE PUIS

# AT THE NOON OF THE DAY

*Lord of all eagerness, Lord of all faith,*
*Whose strong hands were skilled at the plane and the lathe*
*Be there at our labours, and give us, we pray,*
*Your strength in our hearts, Lord, at the noon of the day.*

## *The Angelus*

The Angel of the Lord declared unto Mary;
And she conceived by the Holy Spirit.

Hail Mary, full of grace, the Lord is with thee, blessed art thou amongst women, and blessed is the fruit of thy womb, Jesus.
Holy Mary, Mother of God, pray for us sinners, now and at the hour of our death. Amen.

Behold the handmaid of the Lord;
Be it done unto me according to your word.
Hail Mary …

And the word was made flesh;
And dwelt amongst us.
Hail Mary …

Pray for us, O Holy Mother of God:
That we may be made worthy of the promises of Christ.

Let us pray.

Pour forth, we beseech you, O Lord, your grace into our hearts, that we to whom the incarnation of Christ, your Son, was made known by the message of an angel, may be brought by his passion and cross to the glory of his resurrection, through the same Christ our Lord. Amen.

*St Patrick's Breastplate*

Christ be with me,
Christ within me,
Christ behind me,
Christ before me,
Christ beside me,
Christ to win me,
Christ to comfort
and restore me,
Christ beneath me,
Christ above me,
Christ in quiet,
Christ in danger,
Christ in hearts
of friend and stranger.

O my Lord, how liberal you are and how rich are they to whom you will vouchsafe to be a friend.

*Mary Ward, 1585-1645*

Come, my way, my truth, my life,
Such a way as gives us breath,
Such a truth as ends all strife,
Such a life as killeth death.

Come my light, my feast, my strength,
Such a light as shows a feast,
Such a feast as mends in length,
Such a strength as makes his guest.

Come, my joy, my love, my heart,
Such a joy as none can move,
Such a love as none can part,
Such a heart as joys in love.

*George Herbert, 1593-1633*

*The Prayer of St Ignatius*

Teach us, dear Lord,
to be generous,
to serve you as you deserve to be served,
to give and not to count the cost;
to fight and not to heed the wounds;
to toil and not to seek for rest;
to labour and not to ask for any reward
save that of knowing that we do your will.
Amen.

Lord, make me an instrument of your peace;
Where there is hatred let me sow love,
Where there is injury, pardon;
Where there is doubt, faith;
Where there is despair, hope;
Where there is darkness, light;
Where there is sadness, joy.

O divine master, grant that I may not so much seek
To be consoled, as to console,
To be understood, as to understand,
To be loved, as to love;
For it is in giving that we receive;
It is in pardoning, that we are pardoned,
And it is in dying that we are born to eternal life.

*St Francis of Assisi, 1181-1226*

Lord, open our eyes, that we may see you in our brothers and sisters.

Lord, open our ears, that we may hear the cries of the hungry, the cold, the frightened and the oppressed.

Lord, open our hearts, that we may love each other as you love us.

Renew in us your spirit.

Lord, free us and make us one.

*Mother Teresa, 1910-1997*

Help us to help you.

*A Poet*

Lord, teach me to consider the consequences of my actions. Amen.

*A Poet*

Lord Jesus, help us to make the right choices in life, so we will be able to make the world a better place by being true to each other and to you. Amen.

*A Syntaxian*

Lord, let that be possible for me by your grace which seems impossible to me by nature.

*Mary Ward, 1585-1645*

Lord Jesus, in times of upset we lean on you.
In times of joy, we thank you.
In times of need, we turn to you.
With your goodness and guidance you show us the way.

*A Syntaxian*

*Prayers for our daily work*

Whatever your work is, put your heart into it as if it were for the Lord and not for men, knowing that the Lord will repay you by making you his heirs. It is Christ the Lord that you are serving.

*Colossians 3:23-24*

Our gifts differ according to the grace given us. Use your gift as faith suggests.

*Romans 12:6*

Whatever you do, do it for the glory of God.

*I Corinthians 10:31*

God our Father,
you have placed all the powers of nature under the control of man and his work.
May we bring the spirit of Christ to all our efforts and work with our brothers and sisters at our common task, establishing true love and guiding your creation to perfect fulfillment.

*ICEL*

Lord, give me the grace to work to bring about the things that I pray for.

*St Thomas More, 1478-1535*

*Consecration of Studies – in honour of the Immaculate Conception of the BVM*

Under thy protection dearest Mother, and under the invocation of thy Immaculate Conception do I wish to pursue my studies: and I declare that I study chiefly from this motive, that I may be the better able to assist in spreading God's glory. I beseech thee, therefore, most loving Mother, Seat of Wisdom, to favour and assist my work: and whatever good success I may obtain, I promise on my part, as is but just, to attribute it all to thy intercession with God. Amen.

*Old Stonyhurst Prayer*

Lord, may everything we do
begin with your inspiration
and continue with your help,
so that all our prayers and works may begin in you,
and by you be happily ended.

*From the Roman Missal*

Show, O Lord, thy ways to me,
and teach me thy paths.
Direct me in thy truth, and teach me;
for thou art God my Saviour.

*Blessed Pierre Favre SJ, 1506-46*

# Stations of the Cross

*The congregation pauses for a meditation at each station, which is preceded by this prayer:*

We adore you O Christ, and we praise you.
Because by your holy cross you have redeemed the world.

*The meditation is followed by:*

I love you Jesus, my love, above all things;
I repent with my whole heart for having offended you.
Never permit me to separate myself from you again.
Grant that I may love you always,
and then do with me what you will.

## I

### *Jesus is condemned to Death*

Pilate passes the death sentence on an innocent man because he fears the people and the report they might make about him . . . And so we pray, give us, Lord, the strength to do what is right, no matter what others think or say.

## II

### *Jesus receives the Cross*

There is no need for the soldiers to force the cross on Jesus, because he accepts it gladly for our sakes . . . And so, help me, Lord, when you ask me to carry a cross for my own salvation to accept it with some of the love you showed for me.

## III

*Jesus falls the first time under his Cross*

Human weakness brings Christ to his knees, divine love gets him to his feet again, to struggle on to Calvary. Let me never forget, Lord, that, when my human weakness makes me fall into sin, your supernatural love is there to bring me to my feet again.

## IV

*Jesus is met by his afflicted Mother*

All the sadness of a son and a mother seeing each other suffer, yet bringing each other the strength of love. May I, Lord, never run away from another's sorrow, if I can bring a little comfort and love into that person's life.

## V

*Simon of Cyrene takes up the Cross of Jesus*

How loath Simon must have been, at first, to pick up the cross of salvation! Help us to realise, Lord, that we are apostles in the world, that we can work at your side and bring your salvation to others, by our words and our example.

## VI

### *Veronica wipes the face of Jesus*

A woman breaks through the crowd, and braves the execution squad, to bring him a little relief! Lord, why do I often hang back, when there is some good I can do, some friend I can help? Help me to realise, that a dozen times a day, I can do as much for others as Veronica did for you.

## VII

### *Jesus falls the second time*

With every step Jesus takes, the path gets harder, the burden heavier, the weight of our sins more crushing. And so I pray, Lord, that in my path through life, help me to find my sins harder, not easier, to live with.

## VIII

### *The Women of Jerusalem mourn for Our Lord*

These women cried tears of pity. They had heard marvellous things of this man, but now, he appeared before them, broken and humiliated. Lord, the world today sees you as a failure and your Church as irrelevant. Give me the grace to open peoples' eyes to the truth, to your reality as their Saviour.

## IX

*Jesus falls for the third time*

This time it looks like a complete collapse, the end of the journey. There are times in my life, when I say, 'This is too much, too hard'. May the picture of you, struggling up from this fall, be with me then.

## X

*Jesus is stripped of his garments*

Humiliation and pain. The humiliation of public nakedness, the pain of wounds reopened, as the bandage of your garments is ripped from them. May I find, Lord, in your nakedness, shame for my sins, and see clearly, in your wounds, the pain that I have deserved but that you have felt.

## XI

*Jesus is nailed to the Cross*

The Cross was a symbol of shame and failure, yet the touch of Christ has made it a sign of love and hope. So Lord, may I see the details of my life, not by the world's standards of success and failure, but by whether they are transformed by the touch of your love.

## XII

*Jesus dies on the Cross*

Jesus came to do the will of the Father, and only when he can say with confidence 'It is all done!' does he bow his head and die. And so I pray, Lord, teach me in my life to love God's will, and at the moment of my death, be with me and speak with me your own dying words, 'Father, into your hands I commend my spirit'.

## XIII

*Jesus is taken down from the Cross*

The lifeless body of Jesus is placed in his mother's arms, and Mary suffers the cold shock of emptiness that comes with the death of a dear one. How cold we should feel, if we ever lose Christ by serious sin! So we ask you, Mother of Sorrows, to let us feel, in some small measure, your own sense of loss, if ever we should need it.

## XIV

*Jesus is placed in the Tomb*

So should end a story of defeat. A defeat it has been, but not for the one who died. It is the power of sin that has been destroyed by the Lamb of God who takes away the sins of the world. Sin has no lasting power over me, because I am a sinner who is loved and redeemed by my Saviour.

# AT THE EVE OF THE DAY

*Lord of all kindliness, Lord of all grace,*
*Your hands swift to welcome, your arms to embrace,*
*Be there at our homing, and give us, we pray,*
*Your love in our hearts, Lord, at the eve of the day.*

Sweet Sacrament divine! Hid in thy earthly home,
Lo! Round thy lowly shrine, with suppliant hearts we come;
Jesus, to thee our voice we raise, in songs of love and heartfelt praise,
Sweet Sacrament divine! Sweet Sacrament divine!

Sweet Sacrament of peace! Dear home of every heart.
Where restless yearnings cease, and sorrows all depart;
There in thine ear, all trustfully, we tell our tale of misery,
Sweet Sacrament of peace! Sweet Sacrament of peace!

Sweet sacrament of rest! Ark from the ocean's roar,
Within they shelter blest, soon may we reach the shore.
Save us, for still the tempest raves; save lest we sink beneath the waves,
Sweet Sacrament of rest! Sweet Sacrament of rest!

Sweet Sacrament divine! Earth's light and jubilee,
In thy far depths doth shine, thy Godhead's majesty.
Sweet light, so shine on us, we pray, that earthly joys may fade away,
Sweet Sacrament divine! Sweet Sacrament divine!

*F. Stanfield, 1835-1914*

Godhead here in hiding, whom I do adore,
Masked by these bare shadows, shape and nothing more;
See, Lord, at thy service low lies here a heart
Lost, all lost in wonder at the God thou art.

Seeing, touching, tasting are in thee deceived;
How says trusty hearing? That shall be believed;
What God's son hath told me, take for truth I do;
Truth himself speaks truly, or there's nothing true.

On the cross thy Godhead made no sign to men;
Here thy very manhood steals from human ken;
Both are my confession, both are my belief,
And I pray the prayer of the dying thief.

I am not like Thomas, wounds I cannot see,
But can plainly call thee Lord and God as he;
This faith each day deeper be my holding of,
Daily make me harder hope and dearer love.

O thou our reminder of Christ crucified,
Living Bread, the life of us for whom he died,
Lend this life to me then; feed and feast my mind,
There be thou the sweetness man was meant to find.

Jesu, whom I look at shrouded here below,
I beseech thee send me what I long for so,
Some day to gaze on thee face to face in light
And be blest for ever with thy glory's sight.

Adoro Te Devote, *St Thomas Aquinas, 1227-74*
*tr. Gerard Manley Hopkins SJ, 1844-89*

*Anima Christi*

Soul of Christ, be my sanctification,
Body of Christ, be my salvation,
Blood of Christ, fill my veins.
Water from the side of Christ, wash out my stains.
May Christ's Passion strengthen me,
O good Jesus, hear me.
In thy wounds I fain would hide,
Never to be parted from thy side.
Guard me when my foes assail me,
Call me when my life should fail me.
Command me then to come to thee.
That I for all eternity
With thy saints may praise thee.

*tr. Cardinal John Henry Newman, 1801-1890*

*Guide me, O though great Redeemer*

Guide me, O thou great Redeemer,
Pilgrim through this barren land;
I am weak, but thou art mighty,
Hold me with thy powerful hand:
Bread of heaven,
Feed me till I want no more.

Open now the crystal fountain,
Whence the healing stream doth flow;
Let the fire and cloudy pillar
Lead me all my journey through:
Strong deliverer,
be thou still my strength and shield.

When I tread the verge of Jordan,
Bid my anxious fears subside;
Death of death, and hell's destruction,
Land me safe on Canaan's side:
Songs of praises,
I will ever give to thee.

*tr. W. Williams, 1717-1791 and P. Williams, 1723-1795*

*Salve Regina*

Hail, Holy Queen, Mother of Mercy,
Hail our life, our sweetness and our hope!
To thee do we cry, poor banished children of Eve;
To thee do we send up our sighs,
Mourning and weeping in this vale of tears.
Turn, then, most gracious advocate,
Thine eyes of mercy towards us;
And after this our exile, show unto us
The blessed fruit of thy womb, Jesus.
O clement, O loving, O sweet Virgin Mary.

Pray for us, O holy Mother of God:
That we may be made worthy of the promises of
Christ.

Salve Regina, Mater misericordiæ;
Vita, dulcedo, et spes nostra, salve.
Ad te clamamus, exsules, filii Hevæ.
Ad te suspiramus gementes et flentes
In hac lacrimarum valle.
Eia ergo, Advocata nostra,
Illos tuos misericordes oculos ad nos converte.
Et Jesum, benedictum fructum ventris tui,
Nobis post hoc exilium ostende.
O clemens, O pia, O dulcis Virgo Maria.

*The Memorare*

Remember, O most loving Virgin Mary, that it is a thing unheard of, that anyone ever had recourse to your protection, implored your help, or sought your intercession, and was left forsaken. Filled therefore with confidence in your goodness, I fly to you, O Mother, Virgin of virgins. To you I come, before you I stand, a sorrowful sinner. Despise not my poor words, O Mother of the Word of God, but graciously hear and grant my prayer. Amen.

*Regina Cæli*

Regina Cæli, lætare, alleluia.
Quia quem meruisti portare, alleluia,
Resurrexit, sicut dixit, alleluia,
Ora pro nobis Deum, alleluia.

Joy fill your heart, O Queen most high, alleluia!
Your son who in the tomb did lie, alleluia!
Has risen as he did prophesy, alleluia!
Pray for us, Mother, when we die, alleluia!
Alleluia, alleluia, alleluia!

*tr James Quinn SJ*

*The Rosary*

*The Joyful Mysteries*
The Annunciation
The Visitation
The Birth of Jesus in Bethlehem
The Presentation of our Lord in the Temple
The Finding of Jesus in the Temple

*The Mysteries of Light*
The Baptism of the Lord
The Wedding Feast at Cana
The Proclamation of the Kingdom of God and the Call to Conversion
The Transfiguration
The Institution of the Eucharist

*The Sorrowful Mysteries*
The Agony in the Garden
The Scourging at the Pillar
The Crowning with Thorns
The Carrying of the Cross by Jesus
The Crucifixion and Death of Jesus

*The Glorious Mysteries*
The Resurrection
The Ascension
The Coming of the Holy Spirit upon Our Lady and the Apostles
The Assumption
The Crowning of Our Lady as Queen of Heaven

*Act of Consecration to Our Lady of Lourdes*

Holy Mary, Mother of God, Our Lady Immaculate, you deigned to appear eighteen times at Lourdes for the salvation and consolation of the world. Filled with gratitude and love for you, Mother most kind, I now consecrate myself to your service and the service of your Divine Son.

Help me to be fervent in prayer and to lead an exemplary life; help me to render service to the sick and to pray for the conversion of sinners so that I may work with you and with your Divine Son for the salvation of souls, the peace of the Church and the peace of the world. Amen.

*Blessed be the Holy and Immaculate Conception of Our Lady, Mother of God.*
*Our Lady of Lourdes, pray for us.*
*Saint Bernadette, pray for us.*
*Saint Benedict Joseph Labre, pray for us.*

*Catholic Association*

Hail, Queen of heaven, the ocean star!
Guide of the wanderer here below:
Thrown on life's surge, we claim thy care,
Save us from peril and from woe.
Mother of Christ, star of the sea,
Pray for the wanderer, pray for me.

O gentle, chaste, and spotless Maid,
We sinners make our prayers through thee;
Remind thy Son that he has paid
The price of our iniquity.
Virgin most pure, star of the sea,
Pray for the sinner, pray for me.

Sojourners in this vale of tears,
To thee, blest advocate, we cry;
Pity our sorrows, calm our fears,
And soothe with hope our misery.
Refuge in grief, star of the sea,
Pray for the sinner, pray for me.

And while to him who reigns above,
In Godhead one, in persons three,
The source of life, of grace, of love,
Homage we pay on bended knee;
Do thou, bright Queen, star of the sea,
Pray for thy children, pray for me.

*John Lingard, 1771-1851*

Mother Mary,
Be for me an example of surrender and engagement.
Create within me a heart that is honest and pure,
a heart that offers a haven to others,
a heart that is generous and resolute,
ever able to overcome difficulties,
always ready to begin again,
a humble heart
that expects everything from Jesus
your son and our Lord.
Amen.

*Prayer to Our Lady in the Jesuit Community in Bruges*

My Queen and my Mother, to thee I offer myself without any reserve; and to give thee a mark of my devotion, I consecrate to thee again, my eyes, my ears, my mouth, my heart, and my whole person. Since I belong to thee, O my good Mother, preserve and defend me as thy property and possession.

*The Sodality Prayer*

*Friendship*

Dear Lord,
help me to be patient
even when all I want to do is leave.
Help me to listen even
when all I want to do is talk.
Give me the strength to be
someone else's support.
And see me on my way to being a better friend.
Amen.

*A Rhetorician*

*A Prayer for the Jesuit family*

Lord, in your providence, you guided Saint Ignatius to found the Society of Jesus. Enrich it, we pray, with the gifts of heart, mind and spirit. Make us all one with you in holiness and love, so that we may know your word and obey it as your faithful servants. We ask this through Christ our Lord. Amen.

*From the supplement to the Roman Missal*

Lord, our families are very important to us but sometimes we do not appreciate them as much as we should. We thank you for our loving families and pray that they are well at this time. It may be hard to show we appreciate them at times, but help us show them we love them.

*A Poet*

## Litany of Loretto:
## Order of Service for Benediction

*Hymn*

O salutaris hostia,
Quae cæli pandis ostium;
Bella premunt hostilia,
Da robur, fer auxilium.

Uni Trinoque Domino
Sit sempiterna gloria,
Qui vitam sine termino
Nobis donet in patria.

Amen.

*We fly to thy patronage, O holy Mother of God, despise not our petitions in our necessities, but deliver us from all dangers, O glorious and blessed Virgin.*

| | |
|---|---|
| *Lord, have mercy on us* | **Lord, have mercy on us** |
| *Christ have mercy on us* | **Christ, have mercy on us** |
| *Lord, have mercy on us* | **Lord, have mercy on us** |
| *Christ hear us* | **Christ, graciously hear us** |
| *God, the Father of heaven* | **Have mercy on us** |
| *God, the Son, Redeemer of the world* | **Have mercy on us** |
| *God, the Holy Spirit* | **Have mercy on us** |
| *Holy Trinity, one God* | **Have mercy on us** |

*The Celebrant recites the following invocations and after each the congregation replies* **Pray for us.**

Holy Mary
Holy Mother of God
Holy Virgin of virgins
Mother of Christ
Mother of divine grace
Mother most pure
Mother most chaste
Mother inviolate
Mother undefiled
Mother most amiable
Mother most admirable
Mother of good counsel
Mother of our Creator
Mother of our Saviour
Virgin most prudent
Virgin most venerable
Virgin most renowned
Virgin most powerful
Virgin most merciful
Virgin most faithful
Mirror of Justice
Seat of wisdom
Cause of our joy
Spiritual vessel
Vessel of honour
Singular vessel
of devotion
Mystical Rose
Tower of David
Tower of ivory
House of gold
Ark of the covenant
Gate of heaven
Morning star
Health of the sick
Refuge of sinners
Comfort of the afflicted
Help of Christians
Queen of Angels
Queen of Patriarchs
Queen of Prophets
Queen of Apostles
Queen of Martyrs
Queen of Confessors
Queen of Virgins
Queen conceived
without original sin
Queen assumed into
heaven
Queen of the most holy
rosary
Queen of peace
Queen of the family

*Lamb of God, you take away the sins of the world.*
**Spare us, O Lord.**
*Lamb of God, you take away the sins of the world.*
**Graciously hear us, O Lord.**
*Lamb of God, you take away the sins of the world.*
**Have mercy on us.**
*Pray for us O holy Mother of God.*
**That we may be made worthy of the promises of Christ.**
*Grant, we beseech thee, O Lord, that we thy servants may enjoy perpetual health of mind and body; and by the glorious intercession of the blessed Mary ever virgin, may be delivered from present sorrow and possess eternal joy. Through Christ our Lord.* **Amen.**

*Hymn*
Tantum ergo Sacramentum
Veneremur cernui:
Et antiquum documentum
Novo cedat ritui:
Præstet fides supplementum
Sensuum defectui.

Genitori, Genitoque
Laus et iubilatio,
Salus, honor, virtus quoque
Sit et benedictio:
Procedenti ab utroque
Compar sit laudatio. Amen.

*You have given your people bread from heaven.*
**The bread which is full of all goodness.**

*O God, in this wonderful sacrament you have given us a memorial of your passion. Grant that we may so reverence the sacred mysteries of your Body and Blood that we may always experience within ourselves the effects of the redemption. You who live and reign for ever and ever.* **Amen.**

*The Divine Praises*
Blessed be God,
Blessed be his holy name,
Blessed be Jesus Christ, true God and true man,
Blessed be the name of Jesus,
Blessed be his most Sacred Heart,
Blessed be his most precious blood,
Blessed be Jesus in the most holy sacrament of the altar,
Blessed be the Holy Spirit, the Paraclete,
Blessed be the great mother of God, Mary most holy,
Blessed be her holy and immaculate conception,
Blessed be her glorious assumption,
Blessed be the name of Mary, virgin and mother,
Blessed be St Joseph, her spouse most chaste,
Blessed be God in his angels and in his saints.

*Recessional Hymn*

*The custom of reciting the Litany of Our Lady on Saturday evenings was specifically requested by Mr Thomas Weld, donor of Stonyhurst to the College, so that the tradition he had known at St Omers would be continued there.*

*Evening Prayers*

In the name of the Father and of the Son and the Holy Spirit. Amen.

O God come to our aid.
O Lord make haste to help us.

*Psalm 137*
I thank you, Lord, with all my heart,
you have heard the words of my mouth.
In the presence of the angels I will bless you.
I will adore before your holy temple.

I thank you for your faithfulness and love
which excel all we ever knew of you.
On the day I called, you answered;
you increased the strength of my soul.

All the rulers on earth shall thank you
when they hear the words of your mouth.
They shall sing of the Lord's ways:
'How great is the glory of the Lord!'

The Lord is high yet he looks on the lowly
and the haughty he knows from afar.
Though I walk in the midst of affliction
you give me life and frustrate my foes.

You stretch out your hands and save me,
your hand will do all things for me,
your love, O Lord, is eternal,
discard not the work of your hands.

*Scripture reading*

*The Magnificat*

My soul glorifies the Lord,
my spirit rejoices in God, my saviour.
He looks on his servant in her lowliness;
henceforth all ages will call me blessed.

The Almighty works marvels for me.
Holy his name!
His mercy is from age to age,
on those who fear him.

He puts forth his arm in strength
and scatters the proud-hearted.
He casts the mighty from their thrones
and raises the lowly.

He fills the starving with good things,
sends the rich away empty.

He protects Israel, his servant,
remembering his mercy,
the mercy promised to our fathers,
to Abraham and his sons for ever.

*Luke 1:46-55*

*Pater noster*

Pater noster, qui es in cælis;
sanctificetur nomen tuum;
adveniat regnum tuum;
fiat voluntas tua,
sicut in cælo et in terra.
Panem nostrum quotidianum da nobis hodie;
et dimitte nobis debita nostra, sicut et nos dimittimus debitoribus nostris;
et ne nos inducas in tentationem,
sed libera nos a malo.

We thank you for showing us your mercy today; may that mercy extend to all those whom you entrust to our prayer; and may it bring your peace to all people.

May the souls of the faithful departed through the mercy of God rest in peace.

May God light the fire of his love in our hearts.

Amen.

# AT THE END OF THE DAY

*Lord of all gentleness, Lord of all calm,*
*Whose voice is contentment, whose presence is balm,*
*Be there at our sleeping, and give us, we pray,*
*Your peace in our hearts, Lord, at the end of the day.*

*Psalm 4*

When I call, answer me, O God of justice;
from anguish you released me, have mercy and hear me!
You rebels, how long will your hearts be closed,
will you love what is futile and seek what is false?

It is the Lord who grants favours to those whom he loves;
the Lord hears me whenever I call him.
Fear him; do not sin: ponder on your bed and be still.
Make justice your sacrifice and trust in the Lord.

'What can bring us happiness?' many say.
Lift up the light of your face on us, O Lord.
Let the light of your face shine on us, O Lord.

You have put into my heart a greater joy than they have
from abundance of corn and new wine.

I will lie down in peace and sleep comes at once
for you alone, Lord, make me dwell in safety.

*Prayer of St Richard of Chichester*

Thanks be to you, my Lord Jesus Christ,
for all the benefits and blessings
which you have won for me,
for all the pains and insults
which you have borne for me.
O most merciful Redeemer, friend and brother;
may I know you more clearly,
love you more dearly
and follow you more nearly,
day by day.

*Before Confession*

Almighty and merciful God, you have brought me here in the name of your Son to receive your mercy and grace in my time of need.

Open my eyes to see the evil I have done.

Touch my heart and convert me to yourself.

Where sin has separated me from you, may your love unite me to you again; where sin has brought weakness, may your power heal and strengthen; where sin has brought death, may your Spirit raise to new life.

Give me a new heart to love you, so that my life may reflect the image of your Son.

May the world see the glory of Christ revealed in your Church, and come to know that he is the one whom you have sent, Jesus Christ, your Son, Our Lord. Amen.

Lord, I do not do wrong to hurt you. I do wrong because I am lost, lost in a world that will keep getting darker till someone comes to show me the way. Help me to always stay in your light; within your light there is no dismay.

*A Syntaxian*

*Acts of Contrition*

I love you Jesus, my love above all things. I repent with my whole heart for ever having offended you. Never permit me to separate myself from you again, but grant that I may love you always, and then do with me what you will.

O my God, because you are so good, I am very sorry that I have sinned against you and with the help of your grace I will not sin again.

Lord, you must give us new hearts,
tender hearts, sensitive hearts,
to replace hearts that are made
of marble and bronze.
Place your Heart deep in the centre of our hearts
and enkindle in each heart a flame of love ...
O holy Heart of Jesus, dwell hidden in my heart,
so that I may live only in you and only for you,
so that, in the end, I may live with you eternally in heaven.

*St Claude la Colombière SJ, 1641-1682*

I'm not sure why you take them away, or what you do with them when they're gone. All I ask of you today is that till my time comes to leave you keep them safe.

*A Syntaxian*

We seem to give them back to you, O God, who gave them to us. Yet as you did not lose them in giving, so we do not lose them by their return. Not as the world gives, do you give, O lover of souls. What you give you do not take away, for what is yours is ours if we are yours. And life is eternal and love immortal, and death is only an horizon, and an horizon is nothing save the limit of our sight. Lift us up, strong Son of God, that we may see further; cleanse our eyes that we may see more clearly; draw us closer to yourself that we may know ourselves to be nearer to our loved ones who are with you. And while you prepare a place for us, prepare us also for that happy place, that where you are we may be also for evermore.

*Bede Jarrett OP, 1881-1934*

May the Lord support us all the day long, until the shadows lengthen, and the evening comes, and the busy world is hushed, and the fever of life is over; then Lord, in your mercy, grant us a safe lodging and peace at the last. Through Christ our Lord. Amen.

*Cardinal John Henry Newman, 1801-1890*

Dear Lord, thank you for this day. Life is your gift to me, and I believe that you constantly seek to communicate your love for me through all creation. As I pause before sleep, help me to see where you have been present to me today that I may be thankful for your loving care; and where I have failed to respond to your presence, for this, Lord, help me to be sorry.

He will conceal you with his wings;
you will not fear the terror of the night.

In the name of the Father and of the Son and the Holy Spirit. Amen.

O God, come to our aid.
O Lord, make haste to help us.

I confess to almighty God,
and to you, my brothers and sisters,
that I have sinned through my own fault
in my thoughts and in my words,
in what I have done,
and in what I have failed to do;
and I ask Blessed Mary, ever virgin,
all the angels and saints,
and you, my brothers and sisters,
to pray for me to the Lord our God.

May almighty God have mercy on us,
forgive us our sins,
and bring us to ever lasting life. Amen.

*Psalm 23*

The living God, my Shepherd is,
I know no care or need:
He guides me where rich pastures grow,
Along the verdant mead,
Where everyday, by pleasant way,
My hungering soul may feed.

He leads me where cool waters flow,
By rippling stream and rill,
Where I may taste the springs of life,
My thirsting spirit fill;
He near me bides and homeward guides
My vagrant heart and will.

I nothing fear; thou art, O Lord,
With me through night and day,
Intent, with shepherd's staff and rod,
To guide me when I stray,
And in the fold thou dost uphold
My fainting heart alway.

And so through all the length of days,
Thy mercy waits on me,
At last within my Father's house,
Thy glory I shall see;
Thee ever more will I adore
Through all eternity.

*tr J Driscoll, SJ*

*Scripture reading*

Save us, Lord, while we are awake, protect us while we sleep, that we may keep watch with Christ and rest with him in peace.

*The Nunc Dimittis*

At last, all powerful Master,
you give leave to your servant
to go in peace, according to your promise.

For my eyes have seen your salvation
which you have prepared for all nations,
the light to enlighten the Gentiles
and give glory to Israel, your people.

Glory be to the Father and to the Son and to the Holy Spirit, as it was in the beginning, is now, and ever shall be, world without end. Amen.

Save us, Lord, while we are awake …

Visit we beseech you, O Lord, this house and family, and drive far from it all snares of the enemy; let your holy Angels dwell herein to keep us in peace, and let your blessings be always upon us: through Christ our Lord. Amen.

May the Lord grant us a quiet night and a perfect end. Amen.

May the Lord bless you and keep you.
May his face shine upon you
And be gracious to you.
May he look upon you with kindness,
And give you his peace.
Amen.

*Numbers 6: 24-27*

# REFLECTIONS

LOVE OF GOD
LOVE OF CHRIST
PRAYER
GRACE
MISSION AND VOCATION
JUSTICE
GRATITUDE

Keep your soul in peace.
Let God work in you.
Welcome thoughts that raise your heart to God.
Open wide the window of your soul.

*Letter of St Ignatius Loyola to Antonio de Aroaz SJ*

Nothing is more practical than finding God,
that is,
than falling in love in a quite absolute final way.
What you are in love with,
what seizes your imagination,
will affect everything.
It will decide what will get you out of bed in the morning,
how you will spend your evenings,
how you will spend your weekends,
what you will read, whom you know,
what breaks your heart,
and what amazes you with joy and gratitude.
Fall in love, stay in love,
and it will decide everything.

*Pedro Arrupe SJ, 1907-1991*

Those who love God completely find help in all things; everything supports them in their deserving efforts and in their approach to, and union with, the Creator and Lord himself through their intense love.

*St Ignatius Loyola, Letter to St Francis Borgia 1545 (no.101) cf. Rom 8.28*

Our courteous Lord does not want his servants to despair because they fall often and grievously; for our falling does not hinder him in loving us.

*Julian of Norwich,* Revelations of Divine Love

Love consists in sharing
what one has
and what one is
with those one loves.

Love ought to show itself in deeds
more than in words.

*St Ignatius Loyola,* The Spiritual Exercises *[230]*

I see his blood upon the rose
And in the stars the glory of his eyes.
His body gleams amid eternal snows,
His tears fall from the skies.

I see his face in every flower;
The thunder and the singing of the birds
Are but his voice – and craven by his power.
Rocks are his written words.

All pathways by his feet are worn,
His strong heart stirs the ever beating sea,
His crown of thorns is twined with every thorn,
His cross is every tree.

*Joseph Mary Plunkett OS, 1888-1916*

*The Windhover*

*To Christ Our Lord*

I caught this morning morning's minion, king-
dom of daylight's dauphin, dapple-dawn-drawn
    falcon, in his riding
Of the rolling level underneath him steady air, and
    striding
High there, how he rung upon the rein of a wimpling
    wing
In his ecstasy! then off, off forth on swing,
As a skate's heel sweeps smooth on a bow-bend: the
    hurl and gliding
Rebuffed the big wind. My heart in hiding
Stirred for a bird, – the achieve of, the mastery of the
    thing!

Brute beauty and valour and act, oh, air, pride,
    plume here
Buckle! AND the fire that breaks from thee then, a
    billion
Times told lovelier, more dangerous, O my chevalier!

No wonder of it: sheer plod makes plough down sillion
Shine, and blue-bleak embers, ah my dear,
Fall, gall themselves, and gash gold-vermilion.

*Gerard Manley Hopkins SJ, 1844-1889*

## *The Nature of Prayer*

This Association Prayer Book is intended to help those who use it, to understand more deeply the nature of prayer. It contains, for the most part, other people's prayers but the hope is that it will stimulate prayer as something personal and not necessarily stop the user short at the recital and repetition of what others have said.

Many of us would begin any definition of prayer with the words we heard when we were young, words about lifting our minds and hearts to God. A seventeenth-century Welsh poet, Henry Vaughan, has a wonderful line about prayer as 'the world in tune'. St Ignatius says that it is 'speaking exactly as one friend speaks to another, or as a servant speaks to a master, now asking him a favour, now blaming himself for some misdeed, now making known his affairs to him and seeking advice in them'. The definitions abound, but they will have much in common, principally that prayer is a natural thing for us to undertake, given the relationship that God has to us and we to him.

That is not to say that praying is automatically easy or that it should always seem to us successful or comforting. Prayer has to be honest and genuine and so there will be times when someone else's words cannot possibly be expected to hit off our feelings. This is most likely to be the case when we are bewildered or embittered or downright angry, and at times like that we probably feel that we are in no mood to pray or even that we have no right to try. That would be a great mistake, a classic temptation to set aside.

God, they say, is a wonderful listener and he would have us be listeners too. Jesus told us that, in prayer, we should not be great babblers, not reliant on great floods of eloquence, but simply truthful. (Matt. 6: 7). To pray is to show that we trust the God who always listened and who has given us the right to turn to him at all times. If this little book can help that happen, then it will be a useful book indeed.

*M K O'Halloran SJ*
*The Stonyhurst Association Prayer Book 1993*

Love to pray, since prayer enlarges the heart until it is capable of containing God's gift of himself. Ask and seek and your heart will grow big enough to receive him as your own.

Prayer leads to …
Faith leads to …
Love leads to …
Service leads to …
Peace.

*Mother Teresa, 1910-1997*

As kingfishers catch fire, dragonflies draw flame;
As tumbled over rim in roundy wells
Stones ring; like each tucked string tells, each hung bell's
Bow swung finds tongue to fling out broad its name;
Each mortal thing does one thing and the same:
Deals out that being indoors each one dwells;
Selves – goes itself; *myself* it speaks and spells,
Crying *What I do is me: for that I came.*

I say more: the just man justices;
Keeps grace: that keeps all his goings graces;
Acts in God's eye what in God's eye he is –
Christ. For Christ plays in ten thousand places,
Lovely in limbs, and lovely in eyes not his
To the Father through the features of men's faces.

*Gerard Manley Hopkins SJ, 1844-1889*

Do you want to speak the praise of God? Be yourselves what you speak. If you live good lives, you are his praise.

*St Augustine* Sermon 34

Prayer as petition, as meditation or as liturgical act – these are valid concepts, but prayer as the right and normal expression of one's being is not so generally recognised.

*Tom Burns OS, 1906-1996*

We give praise, reverence and service in becoming involved in God's 'project', which is simultaneously the ongoing conversion of our lives and the establishment of his reign in the world.

*Michael Ivens SJ,* Understanding the Spiritual Exercises, *p.29*

When I see the crowds of these regions, the thought comes to me to go to the universities of your country and especially that of Paris. In the Sorbonne, to those who have more knowledge than the desire to use it profitably, I would like to shout how they should reflect on the account God our Lord will demand of them. Should they reflect on the talents that God has given them, they would feel deep in their heart the will of God and they would seek the interests of Jesus more than their own desires, saying, 'Lord, here I am, what would you want me to do? Send me wherever you want me to be'.

*Letter of St Francis Xavier sent from southern India to the Jesuits in Rome, 15.1.1544*

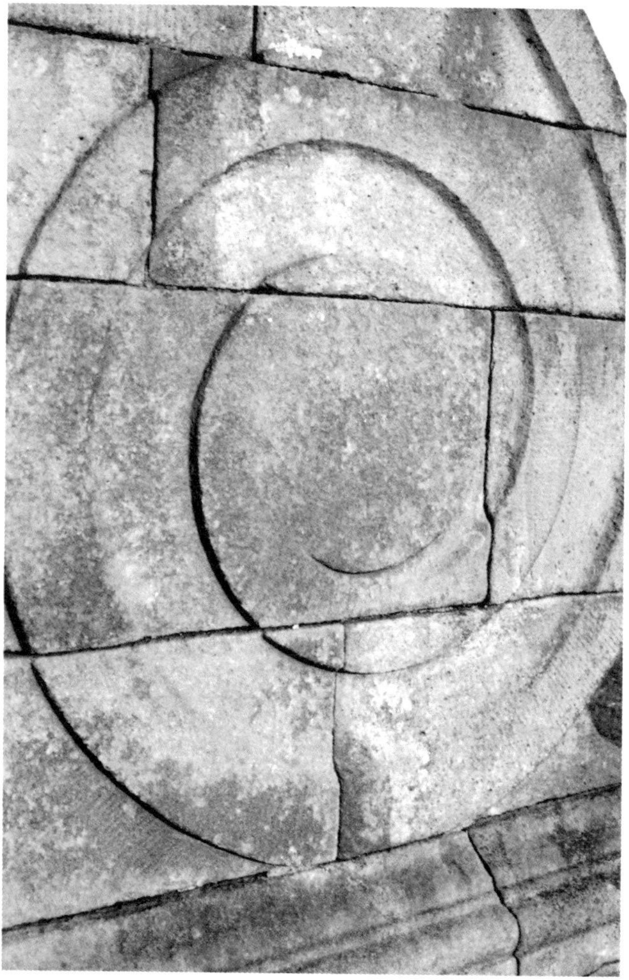

Above all trust in the slow work of God. We are, quite naturally, impatient in everything to reach the end without delay. We should like to skip the intermediate stages. We are impatient of being on the way to something unknown, something new. And yet it is the law of all progress that it is made by passing through some stages of instability – and that it may take a very long time.

And so I think it is with you. Your ideas mature gradually – let them grow, let them shape themselves, without undue haste. Don't try to force them on, as though you could be today what time (that is to say, grace and circumstances acting on your good will) will make you tomorrow.

Only God could say what this new spirit gradually forming within you will be. Give our Lord the benefit of believing that his hand is leading you, and accept the anxiety of feeling yourself in suspense and incomplete.

*Pierre Teilhard de Chardin SJ, 1881-1955*

I have the feeling in our Lord that, just as at one time in our lives we need some particular exercises both spiritual and physical, so at another, different time of our lives we need correspondingly different ones. For what has been good for us at one period is not always such at another.

It is God who sees, and knows what is better for a person, and God knowing everything, shows the person the way forward.

However, for our part, to find that way through the medium of his grace we will be greatly helped if we search about and make many kinds of experiments, so that we can follow the route that he most clearly shows to one, the happiest and most blessed route in this life, completely governed and directed towards that other life, which is without end . . .

*St Ignatius Loyola to St Francis Borgia 20.9.1548*

God has created me to do him some definite service. He has committed some work to me which he has not committed to another. I have my mission. I may never know it in this life, but I shall be told it in the next.

I am a link in a chain, a bond of connection between persons. He has not created me for naught. I shall do good. I shall be an angel of peace, a preacher of truth in my own place while not intending it – if I do but keep his commandments.

Therefore, I will trust him, whatever, wherever I am. I can never be thrown away. If I am in sickness, my sickness may serve him; in perplexity, my perplexity may serve him; if in sorrow, my sorrow may serve him. He does nothing in vain.

*Cardinal John Henry Newman, 1801-1890*

*Consolation*

And the greatest consolation he used to receive was to look at the sky and the stars, which he did often and for a long time, because with this he used to feel in himself a great impetus towards serving Our Lord.

*The Autobiography of St Ignatius Loyola [11]*

For the love of God, do not be slack or half-hearted. As the saying goes, 'Tension may break the bow, but slackness the spirit', and on the contrary 'the soul of the diligent will be richly supplied,' so Solomon tells us. See that you maintain a holy, discriminating verve as you work to acquire both learning and virtue. With both of these one intently performed act is worth more than a thousand done lackadaisically, and what a slacker will not get done in many years, a hard worker will achieve in a short space of time.

In the field of studies the difference between one who works hard and one who is lazy is obvious, but the difference is there too when it comes to overcoming the wild passions and weaknesses that affect our nature and to acquiring virtue. For it is clear that slackers, owing to their failure to struggle against themselves, take longer to attain peace of mind and soul, if indeed they ever do. Nor do they ever completely acquire any of the virtues. By contrast, those who are keen and who work at these things make quick progress, both in studies and also in the personal sphere. Experience shows us that the contentment that can be had in this life is to be found not among the lazy, but rather among those who are bubbling over with keenness for God's service. This stands to reason. These people are making an effort of their own to overcome themselves and get rid of the roots of all wild passions and trouble. Moreover they are acquiring virtues as habits, and so come as a matter of course to act spontaneously and cheerfully in accord with those virtues.

*Letter of St Ignatius Loyola to the Students of Coimbra, Portugal 1547*

Would you honour the body of Christ? Do not despise his nakedness; do not honour him here in church clothed in silk vestments and then pass him unclothed and frozen outside. Remember that he who said, 'This is my body', and made good his words, also said, 'You saw me hungry and gave me no food', and, 'in so far as you did it not to one of these, you did it not to me'. In the first sense the body of Christ does not need clothing but worship from a pure heart. In the second sense it does need clothing and all the care we can give it.

*St John Chrysostom, Homily 50*

Mercy demands that you be merciful, righteousness that you be righteous, so that the creator may be shown forth in the creature and that, in the mirror of man's hearts as in the lines of a portrait, the image of God may be reflected.

*St Leo the Great, Sermon 95*

Men [and women] for others: the paramount objective of Jesuit education . . . must now be to form such men [and women]... this is the prolongation into the modern world of our humanist tradition as derived from the Spiritual Exercises of St Ignatius. Only by being a man for others does one become fully human, not only in the merely natural sense, but in the sense of being the 'spiritual' man of St Paul. He is the man filled with the Spirit; and we know whose Spirit that is: the Spirit of Christ, who gave his life for the salvation of the world; the God who, by becoming man, became, beyond all others, the Man-for-others.

*Pedro Arrupe SJ,* Men for Others

Our ideal is the well rounded person who is intellectually competent, open to growth, religious, loving and committed to doing justice in generous service to the people of God.

*Peter-Hans Kolvenbach SJ, Superior General of the Society of Jesus*

To ask for what I want. Here it will be to ask for interior knowledge of all the good I have received so that acknowledging this with gratitude, I may be able to love and serve his Divine Majesty in everything.

Point 1: This is to bring to memory the benefits received – creation, redemption, and particular gifts – pondering with great affect in how much God Our Lord has done for me, and how much he has given me of what he has; and further, how according to his divine plan, it is the Lord's wish, as far as he is able, to give me himself; and then to reflect and consider within myself what, in all reason and justice, I ought for my part to offer and give to His Divine Majesty . . .

*St Ignatius Loyola,* The Spiritual Exercises *[233, 234]*

Gift better than himself God doth not know;
Gift better than his God no man can see.
This gift doth here the giver given bestow.
Gift to this gift let each receiver be.
God is my gift, himself he freely gave me;
God's gift am I, and none but God shall have me.

*St Robert Southwell SJ, 1561-1595*

**St John Chrysostom** (ca. 349-407): Born at Antioch. After excelling in studies of Philosophy and Rhetoric he spent six years of austerity in the mountains. On his return to Antioch he was ordained and become a renowned preacher, the quality of his sermons giving rise to the name Chrysostom, 'Golden Mouth'. In 397 he became Bishop of Constantinople. His reforming zeal antagonised the powerful of the time, including the imperial court. He was twice exiled and died of exhaustion.

**St Augustine of Hippo** (354-430): Born in Thagaste in North Africa. His studies of Philosophy and Rhetoric lead to an adherence to Manichaeism. In 387 he was converted and was baptised by St Ambrose in Milan. He returned home and founded a community of educated laymen. In 391 he was ordained priest and four years later consecrated Bishop of Hippo. Until his death in 430 he was involved in the major theological controversies of his time.

**St Leo the Great** (d. 461): Born in Tuscany, he became Pope in 440. He was highly influential, both through his pastoral practice and through his teaching, in advancing the primacy of the Bishop of Rome; he played an important role in the doctrinal debates on the nature of Christ, as true God and true man.

**St Francis of Assisi** (1181-1226): Born into a wealthy mercantile family in Assisi, he went on to renounce his carefree high life and his inheritance and adopted a life of poverty and service of the outcast. In 1208 he began to preach the Gospel publicly and gathered around him followers. This new movement, that soon also included women under the inspiration of Clare, was definitively recognised by the Papacy in 1223. Francis was famous for his deep compassion for all people, for his love of creation and for his profound identification with Christ's passion.

**St Richard of Chichester** (1197-1253): Chancellor of Oxford University in 1235. Ordained priest in 1242 after studying with the Dominicans and appointed Bishop of Chichester in 1245. Considered by his contemporaries as a model diocesan bishop. Preached the Crusade towards the end of his life, being canonised in 1262.

**St Thomas Aquinas** (1225-74): Born near Monte Cassino, where he began his schooling, he entered the Dominicans in 1244. He continued his studies in Paris and then at Cologne with St Albert the Great. Although initially held in suspicion he became the outstanding theologian of his day; similar to St Augustine in the extent of his influence on the development of Catholic Theology. Incorporated the thought of Aristotle into his writings.

**Julian of Norwich** (ca. 1342-ca.1420): English mystic who probably lived in isolation outside St Julian's Church, Norwich. Her work, *Sixteen Revelations of Divine Love*, based on a series of visions she received in 1373, has been a lasting influence on theologians stressing the power of the love of God. Her assurance that everything is held in being by the love of God, so that 'all shall be well', has particularly appealed to the contemporary Church.

**St Thomas More** (1478-1535): Lord Chancellor of England, 1529-32. In 1534 refused to swear an oath impugning the Pope's authority and recognising the justice of Henry VIII's divorce from Catherine of Aragon. Beheaded in 1535. Friend of Erasmus and Colet and author of many works in Latin and English, most famously *Utopia*. Beatified in 1886, canonised 1935.

**St Ignatius Loyola** (1491-1556): the youngest son of a noble family of northern Spain, Inigo (as he was baptised) grew up in court circles and aspired to distinguish himself as a soldier in the service of the King of Spain. He underwent a conversion whilst recovering from wounds inflicted at the Battle of Pamplona. His intense desire to help souls led him to renounce his life as a poor pilgrim and to undertake studies in Spain and later in Paris. He gathered around him a group of companions: they put themselves as a body at the disposal of the Pope. So the Society of Jesus was born. Ignatius spent the last years of his life governing the Society from Rome. He is the author of the *Spiritual Exercises*.

**Blessed Pierre Favre** (1506-46): one of Ignatius Loyola's first companions. Born in Savoy, of humble background, he was a promising pupil at school; went to Paris to complete his studies. Shared rooms with Ignatius and Francis Xavier. Undertook the Spiritual Exercises. As a Jesuit he travelled widely in Europe, distinguishing himself as a giver of the Spiritual Exercises and in reconciling those divided by the Reformation.

**St Francis Xavier** (1506-52): Jesuit missionary. A Basque, born in Navarre, he became one of the group of seven who took their vows with Ignatius at Montmartre in 1534. In 1541 he sailed to Goa to evangelise the East Indies and worked in southern India, Ceylon, Malacca, the Molucca Islands and the Malay peninsula. In 1549 he went to Japan and died while on a journey to China.

**Lancelot Andrewes** (1555-1626): Anglican bishop successively of Chichester, Ely and Winchester. Renowned for his patristic learning, he wrote theological works and was first on the list of the divines appointed to produce the Authorised Version of the Bible.

**St Robert Southwell** (1561-95): born in Norfolk, ordained a Jesuit in 1584. From 1586 to 1592 he ran a successful mission in London until his arrest. He was executed in 1595. He was a highly respected poet. Canonised in 1970.

**Mary Ward** (1585-1645): Born into a devout Catholic family in Yorkshire; exposed at an early age to persecution. At 21 went to the Continent and tried her vocation with the Poor Clares. The experience clarified her desire to live an active religious life without cloister; worked in England and on the Continent. With her companions, she founded schools in various European Countries. Encountered opposition to her model of religious life. Founder of the Institute of the Blessed Virgin Mary; the rule, modelled on that of the Society of Jesus, was finally approved in 1703 by Clement XI.

**George Herbert** (1593-1633): one of the outstanding religious poets of the seventeenth century. Educated at Westminster School and at Trinity College, Cambridge, where he later held a fellowship. He was a Canon of Lincoln Cathedral and later Rector of Bemerton, near Salisbury. His collection of poems, *The Temple*, were published after his death.

**St Claude la Colombière** (1641-82): Born on 2 February 1641 at Grenoble, France. Educated at the Jesuit College in Lyons, France, later joining the Society. Preached against Jansenism, advocating dedication to the Scared Heart of Jesus. Spiritual Director of St Margaret Mary Alocoque and chaplain to the Duchess of York. Spent time in England but eventually banished after periods of imprisonment. His health was ruined by prison. Returned to France and died on 15th February 1682 at Paray-le-Monial. Beatified on 16 June 1929 by Pope Pius XI. Canonised on 31 May 1992 by Pope John Paul II.

**Pope Clement XI** (1649-1721): His pontificate dominated by political troubles in Spain, debates around Jansenism in France and the Chinese rites controversy arising out of the activities of the Jesuit missionaries in China.

**Cardinal John Henry Newman** (1801-90): Leading member of the Oxford Movement and author of the Tract XC, in which he argued for the compatibility of the Thirty-Nine Articles with Catholic theology. Joined the Roman Catholic Church in 1845 and became an Oratorian, founding the Birmingham Oratory in 1847.

In 1854 was appointed Rector of the University of Dublin and in 1864 published his *Apologia pro Vita Sua*. Wrote many other works of theology, philosophy, poetry and fiction and in 1879 was created a Cardinal.

**Gerard Manley Hopkins** (1844-89): Converted to Catholicism in 1866. Entered the Jesuit novitiate in 1868 and in 1884 was appointed to the chair of Greek at Dublin University. His poems, none of which were published in his lifetime, were collected by Robert Bridges and published by him in 1918. An enlarged new edition was published in 1967. Hopkins spent five years of his life as a Jesuit at Stonyhurst.

**Pierre Teilhard de Chardin** (1881-1955): French Jesuit paleontologist and theologian. Famous for his speculative use of evolutionary concepts in his theology.

**Bede Jarrett OP,** (1881-1934): a pupil at Stonyhurst from 1891 to 1898. Joined the Dominicans on leaving the College; held the office of Provincial for four successive terms; refounded Blackfriars in Oxford. Described at his death as 'the best known priest in the country'. Famous as a preacher in Britain and the United States.

**Joseph Mary Plunkett,** (1888-1916): was a Philosopher at Stonyhurst from 1906-8. In 1913 he joined the Irish Republican Brotherhood. Was part of the Easter Rising of 1916 and was executed in May of that year.

**Tom Burns,** (1906-1996): a pupil at Stonyhurst from 1922-25; taught by Fr. Martin D'Arcy SJ. A career in publishing brought him to the editorship of *The Tablet*, a responsibility he held from 1967-82.

**Pedro Arrupe** (1907-1991): Superior General of the Society of Jesus (1965-1983); sometimes known as the second Ignatius, being himself a Basque and being instrumental in the renewal of the Society after the Second Vatican Council. Emphasised the need for a faith that does justice; and encouraged Jesuit schools to educate their pupils to be like Christ, men and women for others. As a missionary in Japan he was in Hiroshima the day the atomic bomb was dropped. Helped care for the survivors.

**Mother Teresa**, (1910-1997): Born in Yugoslavia, she began her religious life as a Loretto sister. Sent to Calcutta to teach; she decided to dedicate her life to caring for the poor and in 1949, having left the Loreto sisters, she founded the Missionaries of Charity.

**Thomas Merton** (1915-1968): Poet, novelist, spiritual writer and Trappist monk. Converted to Catholicism in 1938 and joined the Cistercian monastery of Our Lady of Gethsemani, Kentucky in 1941. Wrote many books on aspects of Catholic spirituality, the most famous being his autobiography *The Seven Storey Mountain* and *Seeds of Contemplation*. Died in Bangkok while addressing an international conference of Asian monastics.

## INDEX

LDS

IHS